BLOGGING FOR BUSINESS

OLA OBEMBE

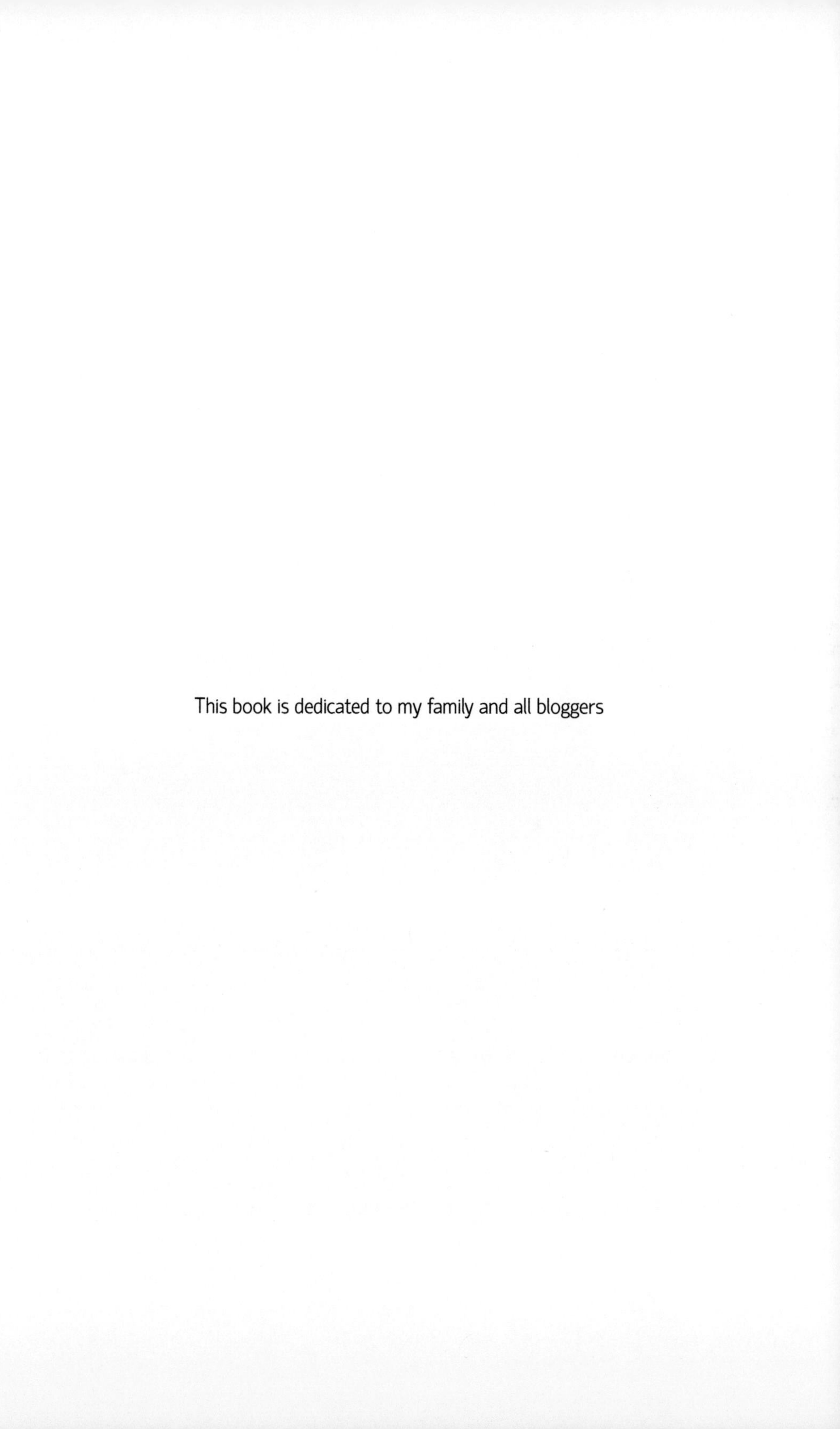

This book is dedicated to my family and all bloggers

Contents

CHAPTER ONE

What Is A Blog

A Blog is defined as a journal that is shared online where you can place your hobbies and interests as well as other items. Yet another way to describe blogging as a way to promote items in a way that is simple and easy. In other words, it can be used as a form of free advertising for anything that the chosen user is either trying to sell or promote. The blog consists of short paragraphs that tell about your product or ideas. There are many reasons why a person would want to create a blog.

One of the most popular reasons though is that you can use your blog to promote your business and not spend any money on advertising. This is a great advantage especially if your business is just starting and you do not have a lot of start-up cash available. It is also good for small businesses, especially home-based businesses, to advertise without needing to spend a lot of their income on advertising. Another great advantage to creating your blog is that you will come across as an expert on the topic you have chosen. Visitors to your blog will just love the information on your blog and feed on that information. They will think you are a genius to know all that you do. This may sound strange but it's true. Many different blog sites are available on the internet today. Blogger is one of the most popular of these. Most of the blog sites will give you a template that you can use to create your site.

The most important thing to remember though when creating your blog is you will need to change it daily or even several times a day. Keep the information current and up to date. The more maintenance you perform to your blog the more visitors that will visit. Also if you create your blog to be SEO compatible, you will attract more visitors to your site. SEO consists of keywords that appear on your website that web crawlers attach onto and feed them back to the search engines. The more keywords you have in your blog, the higher the ranking on the search engine will be. To build a blog on a certain topic of interest you must build a reputation. If you are just using it as a shared journal this is fine but for businesses, reputation is very important. Visitors need to know your reputation to deem you as an expert in the topic of your blog.

Once they deem you as an expert they will keep coming back for more information on your topic. No matter what reason you create your blog it is an excellent way to promote yourself or your business. Blogging For Business Owners If you run a small company, you may find that the world of blogging for business owners is a world that you want to be a part of. Blogging is a great way to get the word out to consumers about your product or service, and it can even be useful for inspiring employee loyalty and helping you keep your workers at peak morale. If you are looking for a way to take your business to the next level, consider what starting a blog might be able to do for you.

Blogging for business owners has a lot in common with all other types of blogging, but it has its unique pitfalls and strengths. The key to having a successful blog as a business owner is keeping your goals clear and concrete at every step of your blogging adventure. It can be all too easy to get sidetracked, especially if you are just learning about the exciting possibilities of blogging technology, but if you want your blog to succeed you need to stay focused. Write up a plan for how often you will update, how you will promote your blog and retain readers, whether you will feature photographs or video, and other aspects of your blog, and then stick to it with the same kind of determination that you used when you built your company.

CHAPTER TWO

How To Build Traffic To Your Website

Website Websites are created to share and provide information to the targeted audiences. The common ingredient in all successful websites is the traffic they attract. Traffic is the key element of all websites. Search engines, recommendations, and directories are very valuable traffic methods.

Search engines are searching for relevant content, keywords, Meta tags, and images. When you have the information on your site you get traffic. Recommendations are precisely what the names state. You receive recommendations from internet users that recommend your site to others. Directories are lists of categories that are grouped for easy access by people searching for information. To achieve traffic from the search engines, you need to have high rankings on their results. It is the same with directories.

Recommendations are achieved by word of mouth from a happy client to another source. You provide a great service or product and word will spread. These are the most popular forms of obtaining website traffic. You may have to pay for some of the services yet to make money you may have to spend money. There are other options to obtain website traffic. You can use organic placement. This is the process of your site being located due to it being found by a copious number of individuals with their search results making your rankings on the search engines rise with each hit as it increases in popularity.

To make increase your organic placement, you use relevant keywords and terms in different phrasing that the internet users may enter into the search engines. You can achieve higher levels of traffic using the first three methods. You will have to work hard to get the traffic. You need to be determined and unyielding with your efforts. It will take time yet once you start seeing the results from your efforts you know you have reached a very high goal you set for your business.

It is something anyone is proud to achieve. Add other simple traffic methods such as newsletters, viewer feedback forums, affiliate marketing, blogging, RSS feeds, and video to your website. There are other methods to make your website more appealing and interesting. Any additional content or features you add to your site will increase your traffic. When you want to attract an audience to your website, you have to have a high-quality interesting, and an intriguing site filled with content other sites don't have.

You have to be the leader in the industry so you stand out on crowded internet websites. It has been said to be a successful businessperson you need to learn to think outside the box. This is true for your website and business. Picking The Best Free Blogging Site Choosing a free blogging site can feel overwhelming because there are so many options. Several large free blog-hosting sites dominate the blogosphere, but there are also smaller sites. Whether you decide to join up with an established site like a blogger or whether you choose to sign on with a relatively new venture depends on what your priorities are.

Reliability is perhaps the best reason to opt for a large and well known free blogging site. When you choose to have an established brand host your blog, you can feel secure that your blog will not crash often and will not disappear in the middle of the night. A company that has been around for a while is likely to have the resources to make sure that its clients aren't unpleasantly surprised by any technical glitches. However, many bloggers decide that this isn't enough of a selling point.

The bloggers who choose to go with smaller, newer blog hosting sites do so for a variety of reasons, but perhaps the number one advantage is a fairly abstract one. Bloggers tend to relish the fact that the internet is a place where the underdog has a strong chance of success, and by choosing to have a small company as a blog host, a blogger is casting his or her vote for David against Goliath. The Right Blogging Platform For Your Needs Choosing which blogging platform to use is one of the most important decisions that you can make as a blogger. The right platform can make blogging a breeze, and the wrong platform can make blogging a chore.

Because the program that you use to blog with is such a powerful part of your blogging experience, it is well worth putting in the time to find a platform that provides your ideal balance between a user-friendly interface and a flexible framework that allows you to make your blog look and feel unique. Finding the right platform isn't always easy, but with a little bit of contemplation and a little bit of research, you will be on your way to finding the perfect blogging platform. Deciding what your priorities are in terms of ease of use versus customization.

Most highly customizable blogging platforms, like moveable type, are a bit more difficult to use than very automated platforms like WordPress. If you are new to blogs and internet technology, you might want to sacrifice the ability to create a custom background design or to integrate a unique font into your template to find a program that will be easy for you to use. On the other hand, if you are a veteran web designer with knowledge of Html or javascript, you will probably find the limitations of a user-friendly platform to be frustrating.

There is no such thing as a blogging platform that is objectively the best because every blogger has unique needs. The blogging movement is very much about individuality, so it makes plenty of sense that there would be many different platforms available that are designed to meet the needs of different kinds of individuals undertaking different kinds of projects.

This diversity is a good thing because it means that you will almost certainly be able to find a program that suits your level of technical aptitude. However, the fact that no two bloggers need the same thing from a blogging platform can make your search for the right platform a bit tricky. When you are reading reviews of different platforms, try to keep your priorities in mind and do your best to take into account the position that the reviewer is coming from.

For example, a negative review written by an accomplished software designer who complains that a popular platform is too limited may tell you that the platform in question is ideal for a beginning blogger. There is no such thing as the perfect platform for everybody, so instead of looking for the "best" platform, look for the best platform for your specific criteria. 5 Common Types Of Business Blogs A blog is a site that a person can use as a live journal or promote a business. When you are promoting a business, however, you will need to do a lot of research on the topic before beginning. If you are new to blogging, as a business, or just want to get the word out on a certain business, you need to know the more common business topics.

This can provide you with a starting point. The five most common businesses use blogs to promote their business.

1. Specialty Blogs This type of business blog is usually written by two more contributes with a common interest. It is a great way for you to build an online community with people that share your interests and ideas. This

type of blog can include things like weight loss, how to stay healthy, or even golf topics among others. The possibilities are endless. 2. Feature Blogs In this type of blog you will be advertising creative types of businesses. These creative topics can include but are not limited to, topics on sewing, crafting, computer programming, and digital photography as well as many others. The possibilities for this type of business blog are endless. In this type of business blog, you have the opportunity to show various pictures, video clips, and even sewing projects that you have been working on among others. This is one type of business blog that you will need to be a creative one. The more creative you are the more visitors you will get.

3. Industry Blogs This blog focuses on a more narrow type of industry and usually is made by industries that sell their products to other businesses. It usually consists of a variety of different topics including trade shows, new lines of product, and materials among others. This is a little more difficult of a blog to create. It will take a lot of careful research and you will need to know a lot of information on the industry you are creating your blog on.

4. Tourist Blogs Of all the business blogs so far this is about the easiest and the most fun to create. You can write on certain tourist areas of interest and include pictures of the area. You can add tourist attractions famous to the area along with the climate and travel information just to name a few.

5. Consulting blogs Usually consulting blogs are run by one person offering their opinion, and advice on a certain topic. This is a great way to develop an online community on a topic that interests you. No matter what business you wish to create or may already belong to, blogging is a great way to advertise.

CHAPTER THREE

Monetizing Blogs

You have been requested to deliver great quality, unique substance on your blog and you have drawn in a nice measure of traffic. Notwithstanding, cash will show up out of nowhere since you have traffic. You need to transform your traffic into cash. There are multiple approaches to produce benefits from the guests of your blog, and Google's Adsense program permits you to do as such no sweat. In the first place, visit their site at http://adsense.google.com/.

You'll discover more with regards to their publicizing program there, yet here are some additional pieces I'd prefer to tell you. To begin with, Google's Adsense program is a truly valuable approach to adapt your blog since when clients wrap up perusing your most current post, odds are they need to leave your blog since they don't have anything else to do on your blog. If your Adsense notice block is apparent on your blog, they may see promotions applicable to them and snap-on them to leave your blog.

You've recently taken advantage of your first virtual pennies! Be that as it may, indeed, your benefits may be pennies if you don't "do it right". This includes putting your Google promotions in the ideal places and guaranteeing they mix into your site so they show up more like connections as opposed to ads to your guests. Counsel the page https://www.google.com/support/adsense/container/static.py?page=tips.html to see the "heat map" of your blog. The "more sweltering" a specific region, the more noteworthy the odds of somebody taking a gander at your blog. When you get a Google Adsense account, you can change the shade of your notice text and connections.

You will need them to coordinate with the shadings on your blog. In case your blog's text is dark and the connections are red, do likewise for the promotion hinders as well! It's just straightforward. One more approach to procuring benefits from your blog is to prescribe items to your customers.

At the point when your guests purchase from the shippers you suggest, you will keep a little commission as well. This is known as member showcasing and it is extremely simple to begin since you don't need to make your items or administrations.

At any rate, we should allude back to our mechanical devices blog model. Suppose you find this Product Y on a trader's site, and they offer an affiliate program. What you would do is to make a post in your blog and complete a smaller than expected survey on this Product Y. Tear it separated and call attention to its advantages and terrible focuses, assuming any, and incorporate a connection (which is given by the dealer) for the guest to buy the Product Y on the web. On the off chance that your guest snaps and buys the contraption, the vendor will follow from the connection that the buy is alluded by you, so they will send you a lot of the benefits.

Envision if 1 out of each 100 guests you get buys this item, and you procure a $24.00 commission from each buy! On the off chance that you get 10,000 guests in a month that would be a $2,400.00 paycheque for you only for expounding on ONE item. Presently, partner programs are extremely pleasant approaches to create benefit, however, how would you discover offshoot programs that are identified with your blog's topic? Simple, simply go to Google and look for +"affiliate programs".

Another somewhat better way is to go to http://www.associateprograms.com/search to search for offshoot programs in your specialty. The two different ways referenced above are fundamental approaches to creating benefits from your blog. Other Monetizing Options We've examined using the Google Adsense program and other traders' associate projects to produce benefits from your blog. In any case, we have a ton of different alternatives to adapt your blog, so we will investigate that today.

The primary alternative we'll be checking out is Chitika (www.chitika.com). Chitika is an extremely imaginative logical promoting program since it can serve exceptionally itemized commercials. For instance, on your mechanical contraption blog, Chitika will show ads for tech devices like iPods. How they show it is in various tabs: one for "Best arrangements", one more for "subtleties", one more for "surveys, etc. Along these lines, it is a greater amount of an enlightening area for your guest instead of a promotion, and normally the navigation will be higher. You can apply here: https://chitika.com/application.php?type=mm

You can likewise be a partner for Amazon.com. Amazon offers a wide scope of items yet its transcendent area is in books. Whatever your specialty is about, you can presumably discover a book about it on Amazon.com. Join their Associate program here: https://associates.amazon.com/gp/flex/partners/apply-login.html/

When you go along with them, you can allude guests to them and procure up to 10% commission. It's anything but a great deal however if you can figure out how to allude to large volumes of guests, Amazon is intended for you. This program truly sparkles with regards to the manners in which you can allude to guests: you can utilize their predefined layouts to pull up late things that match a specific model you set, you can focus on your advertisement to show a particular thing discounted or you can mesh your outside references into your blog entries.

Last but certainly not least, you can sell promoting space on your blog if your blog is genuinely well known. Simply investigate sites like http://xiaxue.blogspot.com. That blog gets more than 10,000 site visits each day and normally vendors will need to hit an arrangement with the blog's proprietor to post their ads there. On the off chance that you figure out how to pull in colossal measures of traffic like that blog, you can get individuals to purchase advertisement space on your blog at costs from $150/month upwards, contingent upon your blog fame.

To measure how many site hits and guests you get regularly, simply utilize the free instrument accessible at www.statcounter.com. They have an exceptionally nitty gritty arrangement guide there so I will not go into it. On the off chance that your blog has not obtained a huge measure of guests yet, you can in any case sell promotion space on your blog for each snap or per impression premise. Simply visit locales like www.adbrite.com. For a total rundown of these locales, visit http://performancing.com/hub/60. Ideally, that will assist you with boosting income and benefits from your blog!

Blogging for Profit Begins With a Long Term Plan Many people dream of blogging for profit, and this goal is not far beyond the reach of someone with average intelligence, a willingness to work hard, and a basic grasp of blogging technology. However, very few people manage to reap the profits they want from their blogs. Most people who attempt to make money with their blogs do not succeed for two reasons. Often, bloggers have unrealistic expectations of how fast their readership will grow and how much money they will make, and when these expectations are not met the disappointment can crush the desire to continue blogging.

The other trap that many bloggers fall into has to do with a lack of planning. If you want to turn a profit as a blogger, the key to success is to make a realistic plan and stick with it. To succeed at blogging for profit, the main thing that you will need is a large readership. The higher your traffic, the more advertisers will agree to pay you. However, cultivating the regular visitors that you will need to make a profit isn't easy. As more and more blogs appear each day, having a great idea or a wonderful writing style is no longer enough to get attention.

You need to be able to market your blog effectively. Too many bloggers spend all of their time writing posts and almost no time marketing their projects. To be certain, updating as often as you can is a great way to keep your blog high on blogrolls and high in blog search engines like technorati, and once your readers know that you update frequently they will return to your site regularly.

However, it does not matter how often you update if nobody is reading your page, so don't skimp on the time that you spend drawing visitors to your site. To make your dreams of blogging for profit a reality, try decreasing your number of posts and using some of that time to draw new visitors by setting up link exchanges with other bloggers, making contacts in the blogging community, and following other established modes of winning traffic. Of course, even if you are a marketing genius or have a great idea for a blog, success is not going to happen overnight. Building the kind of readership that blogging for profit requires takes time, and in all likelihood, it will be at least several months before you can turn much of a profit.

Try to stay committed to your blogging project during this initial rough period. To stay motivated, set goals for how often you will update and how many readers you want to attract, and then reward yourself for sticking with your plan. Learning How to Make Money Blogging There are two major types of business models that entrepreneurs use to make money blogging. The first and most common way to turn a blog into a profit-making machine is to sell advertising to different companies and brands who want to reach that blog's readers.

The second kind of money-making blog helps a single brand improve its image by creating positive associations between the blog and the product in the mind of consumers. Both kinds of blogs can make a lot of money, especially if the creator has a keen mind for marketing. If you are blogging intending to sell advertising, there are two basic ways that you can go about recruiting sponsors who want to put ads on your site; you can let someone else do all of the legwork, or you can do the work yourself and keep all of the revenue. Within the first group, many people make money blogging by selling space through Google's AdSense program.

The advantages of this program are numerous, as it requires very little effort on the part of the blogger or webmaster to begin raking in profits. However, most people discover that they make less money through this method than they had hoped that their blog would earn. Selling advertising directly to companies who want to put banner ads or sponsored links on your blog can take quite a bit of time, but it is often fairly lucrative. If you have a lot of contacts in industries that are related to the topic of your blog, you may want to try to go this route.

People who have a strong background in sales and are experienced at pitching proposals can make quite a bit of money by renting blog space to interested companies. The most serious problem with this model is that you often have to build quite a sizable readership before you can attract advertisers, which can mean that you have to do several months of work before you start to make money blogging. As blogging becomes a more and more lucrative business, a lot of established companies are considering how they can get into the action.

One way that companies are capitalizing on the blog movement is by having blogs that provide a kind of friendly face for their corporation. Often, a company will employ an established blogger to create a weblog designed specifically to appeal to that company's customers and to create positive associations with the brand in consumers' minds. More than one writer who never even dreamed that he or she could make money blogging has been approached by a company and offered quite a pretty penny for this kind of gig.

CHAPTER FOUR

Blogging News Stories as They Happen

Blogging news stories as they unfold is one of the most exciting and controversial applications of technology that bloggers have discovered. One thing that makes the blogosphere so active is the fact that it is possible to update a blog instantaneously, so the news on blogs tends to be more current than the news in the paper, or on television. Unlike news delivered by these other media, news that appears on blogs does not have to travel through a series of editors and administrators before it reaches the public eye.

This has some advantages and some distinct disadvantages. One of the most notable cases of news hitting a blog before appearing in other media took place in July 2005 when terrorism struck London. As passengers were evacuated from a subway car near an explosion, one man took several photographs of the scene with his cellular phone, and within an hour these images were posted online.

First-person accounts of the catastrophe began appearing on blogs soon after these photos appeared, and people all over the world learned about the events in London by reading the words and seeing the photos posted by bloggers. The fact that these stories and images were being spread directly by individuals operating without the added filter of a reporter helped to make the crisis feel very immediate to people across the globe. When it comes to blogging, news often appears in a very personal context.

This has the potential to be the beginning of an exciting new era of reporting, one that takes "New Journalism" to its logical next step by putting the power to shape how the news is written and read directly into the hands of the public. Many bloggers and cultural commentators who are champions of the weblog movement feel that this growing trend of individuals who get their news from blogs is a good thing because it makes the flow of information more democratic. By decentralizing the control of news, blogs allow more voices to enter the field of debate about important current events.

However, many people are adamantly opposed to the use of blogs as news outlets, and there are plenty of good arguments on this side of the debate. Unlike newspapers or television stations, few blogs have fact-checkers, and there is little attention paid to journalistic accountability on many blogs. This can lead to the rapid spread of misinformation, and more than one falsehood has taken the blogosphere by storm.

The questions about whether blogging news as it happens is ethical or not are very complicated, but no matter where you stand on the topic of current events blogs you are almost sure to agree that this movement has the potential to revolutionize how modern people get their news. Picking The Best Free Blogging Site Choosing a free blogging site can feel overwhelming because there are so many options. Several large free blog-hosting sites dominate the blogosphere, but there are also smaller sites. Whether you decide to join up with an established site like a blogger or whether you choose to sign on with a relatively new venture depends on what your priorities are.

Reliability is perhaps the best reason to opt for a large and well known free blogging site. When you choose to have an established brand host your blog, you can feel secure that your blog will not crash often and will not disappear in the middle of the night. A company that has been around for a while is likely to have the resources to make sure that its clients aren't unpleasantly surprised by any technical glitches. However, many bloggers decide that this isn't enough of a selling point. The bloggers who choose to go with smaller, newer blog hosting sites do so for a variety of reasons, but perhaps the number one advantage is a fairly abstract one.

Bloggers tend to relish the fact that the internet is a place where the underdog has a strong chance of success, and by choosing to have a small company as a blog host, a blogger is casting his or her vote for David against Goliath. Offpage Search Engine Optimization Improvement of our blog to rank well for query items of specific watchwords we're targetted, however here comes the tragic news – it influences your positioning is without a doubt, exceptionally minor ways. Be that as it may, don't avoid this progression as every piece helps when you're visiting for web crawler rankings! Presently, we're continuing to off-page website streamlining.

Those are factors that are not on your blog but rather influence your web index rankings significantly. There is a great deal of off-page factors, yet we will concentrate on them individually.

The first and most clear one is the number of connections to your blog. When in doubt of thumb, the more connections to your blog, the more the web crawlers think you are an expert in that specific specialty and thus the higher they rank you. Nonetheless, take care to notice the nature of the connections. For instance, 1,000 connections from absolutely superfluous locales like internet dating destinations would not help at all because your blog is an innovative item blog. Interestingly, a solitary connection from an exceptionally legitimate website about mechanical contraptions will get the web indexes slithering with regards to your blog like the Feds raging a break sanctum...

At any rate, the most practical method of getting great connections from legitimate locales is just to request it. On the off chance that your blog contains top-notch content that is unique and will give significant data to the web page's perusers, chances are the webmaster(s) will connect to your blog or even expound on you! How about we talk regarding how we ought to request these website admins from power to connect to your blog. We're examining this dependent on the assumption that your blog is truly content-rich and deals excellent data to anybody in your specialty or subject of conversation.

The most feasible alternative is to send an email straightforwardly to the website admin. In the first place, we should search for the top locales in your specialty. Essentially scan the significant web crawlers for the term that you're targetting. For this situation, we should look for "mechanical devices". The initial not many outcomes, www.t3.co.uk

and www.acarplace.com/brands/gm/gadgets.html

are business destinations, so try not to inquire.

We're searching for local area-based destinations and different web journals that are more open to a total newbie like you. Seems like www.gizmodo.com would be a decent alternative! Thus, form and email to the website admin of www.gizmodo.com (whose email address you will discover on the webpage). They even have their AIM contact there, so it's additionally a decent decision if you use AOL Instant Messenger. Start by expressing how you went over their site (for example "searching for device data", NOT "searching for connecting accomplices!") and how you think their site gives significant information.

Fundamentally, attempt to say something great with regards to their site genuinely. Then, at that point, recommend that this and that substance on your blog will be a decent supplement to their website's substance as well as the other way around. Put a connection on your blog to their website and ask inconspicuously on the off chance that they could do likewise to weld a commonly helpful connection between the webpage and your blog. En route, you may discover individuals who will not react to your email, so disregard them and continue.

Eliminate the connections from your blog to their webpage if they have not reacted to your email within two weeks, which is a lovely huge delay. Continue to do this for the initial 30 indexed lists that spring up, and after a short time, you ought to have many great locales all connecting to you. In the following article, we will investigate further the further developed off-page variables, and approaches to further develop them! On-Page Search Engine Optimization Presently, you ought to have a blog full of content you have enthusiastically composed.

It ought to be an exceptionally intriguing grapevine for the local area of your picked specialty, rather than a dormant factsheet. Nonetheless, regardless of how tasty your substance is, in case there is no one to peruse it you can't create benefit from it. Traffic is the soul of your blog. To draw in individuals, you should offer alluring data. Sufficiently basic. Notwithstanding, to get traffic onto your site, you need to think in reverse. Where do individuals look when they need data? Indeed, they search utilizing web search tools like www.google.com, www.yahoo.com, and www.msn.com

, to give some examples of more famous ones.

Thus, to get these individuals on your blog, your blog needs to rank high on query item pages of these web indexes. At the point when these individuals look for data through the web crawlers and see your website among the top outcomes, they will normally navigate to your blog! The craft of getting your blog or site onto high rankings on query output pages is called website improvement. It is an exceptionally intricate and hard subject to dominate, yet that doesn't prevent us from learning basic yet compelling procedures to overcome the indexed lists for specific catchphrases.

The more intricate methods are normally expected to battle for exceptionally cutthroat and general watchwords, for example, "fat misfortune", however, I'll show you how to defeat that later. Until further notice, we should decide the watchwords that you need to streamline your site for. For instance, your blog discusses tech devices. Presently, you'd need to check in Google whether it is an extremely competitive catchphrase. During this season of composing, there are 29,000,000 indexed lists.

Figure you can beat 29, 000, 000 destinations at your first endeavor? I don't think so. Presently, how about we attempt to limit our extension. We should search for "innovative contraptions" all things being equal. During this season of composing, Google records 792, 000 outcomes. That is more sensible, however, you'd prefer to look for more engaged catchphrases. Nonetheless, we should upgrade your blog for "innovative contraption" only for learning. In the first place, you need to focus on the title of your blog.

Since you're enhancing for innovative contraptions, you need to have that accurate expression in your blog title. For instance, a line like "Your Best Technological Gadget Blog!" would work extraordinary. You can change the title of your blog in the Blogger control board or the WordPress blog when you're making it. In case you're capable with HTML, you can even do that on other blog motors like Moveable Type. Main concern? Get familiar with a little HTML! Other than that, your page heading ought to likewise contain the term you're upgrading for.

The page heading is the piece of text in your code that is encased inside the labels. This is significant as it advises the web search tools about your page (for this situation, "mechanical devices"). Since we're posting a blog, the labels are typically the post titles, so make sure to incorporate the term there at whatever point is important. One final piece, you ought to likewise sprinkle the words "innovative contraptions" in your posts sooner rather than later. The continuous event of that expression in your blog will indicate the web indexes that your blog is truly pertinent to that point. In any case, this is the main piece of all.

Continuously remember that you're composing for genuine individuals who read your blog to acquire data, so it is exceptionally inept to spam your blog with watchwords! Indeed, on the off chance that you do that, the web indexes will wind up reasoning you're spamming and drop your positioning further down into obscurity... So remember! Compose for people, not web crawlers! Offpage Search Engine Optimization II Getting great connections from legitimate sites in your field can help your internet searcher rankings.

This time, we will investigate further into connecting techniques, and how to decide and get "top caliber" joins. We're additionally going to speak momentarily about Google's PageRank.

To start with, how about we inspect a standard connection. It's a piece of text (or picture, however, we're going for text) that connects to your blog, and a portion of the variables that matter are 1) The location which it connects to 2) The text of the connection 3) The PageRank of the page on which the connection lives How about we investigate this data individually. To start with, you'd normally need the connection to connect to your blog, yet to which page of your blog? To a singular post or your blog's landing page? Since your blog is a continually refreshed site, it is consistently insightful to gather every one of the connections to highlight your primary page all things considered if the individual presents since they tend to be very time-delicate.

The text of the connection additionally influences your rankings for a specific watchword. Suppose your blog is about innovative devices and another website has a connection that says "Barbie dolls" and connections to your blog. Doesn't bode well, correct? If a ton of connections that connect to your site contain the expressions "innovative" or "contraption", it will significantly support your rankings for those catchphrases.

Henceforth, it's crucial to put a few considerations when mentioning joins from different website admins as you need them to connect to your blog with suitable catchphrases. Presently, about Google's PageRank. It's fundamentally a scale set by Google to gauge the prevalence of sites. You can peruse more with regards to it on http://www.google.com/innovation/. Is fascinating that the higher the PageRank of a specific site, the more incessant Google's robots will visit the site to record it. The PageRank of a page will likewise assist it with positioning higher in Google's web index results. So, having a high PageRank will bring you many advantages SEO-wise. Your blog will begin with no PageRank (which is diverse to PageRank 0) since

Google has not yet recorded your blog. When Google's robots discover your blog through joins on different destinations, your blog will show a PageRank of 0, and relying upon the PageRank of the alluding page, your blog's PageRank will likewise rise ultimately. Getting great connections to your blog will help direct targeted guests who are keen on your specialty to your blog, empower web search tools to discover and list your blog, and at last position higher in web crawler results.

CHAPTER FIVE

The Right Blogging Platform For Your Needs

Choosing which blogging platform to use is one of the most important decisions that you can make as a blogger. The right platform can make blogging a breeze, and the wrong platform can make blogging a chore. Because the program that you use to blog with is such a powerful part of your blogging experience, it is well worth putting in the time to find a platform that provides your ideal balance between a user-friendly interface and a flexible framework that allows you to make your blog look and feel unique.

Finding the right platform isn't always easy, but with a little bit of contemplation and a little bit of research, you will be on your way to finding the perfect blogging platform. Deciding what your priorities are in terms of ease of use versus customization. Most highly customizable blogging platforms, like moveable type, are a bit more difficult to use than very automated platforms like WordPress. If you are new to blogs and internet technology, you might want to sacrifice the ability to create a custom background design or to integrate a unique font into your template to find a program that will be easy for you to use. On the other hand, if you are a veteran web designer with knowledge of Html or javascript, you will probably find the limitations of a user-friendly platform to be frustrating.

There is no such thing as a blogging platform that is objectively the best because every blogger has unique needs. The blogging movement is very much about individuality, so it makes plenty of sense that there would be many different platforms available that are designed to meet the needs of different kinds of individuals undertaking different kinds of projects. This diversity is a good thing because it means that you will almost certainly be able to find a program that suits your level of technical aptitude. However, the fact that no two bloggers need the same thing from a blogging platform can make your search for the right platform a bit tricky. When you are reading reviews of different platforms, try to keep your priorities in mind and do your best to take into account the position that the reviewer is coming from.

For example, a negative review written by an accomplished software designer who complains that a popular platform is too limited may tell you that the platform in question is ideal for a beginning blogger. There is no such thing as the perfect platform for everybody, so instead of looking for the "best" platform, look for the best platform for your specific criteria. The Controversy Around Corporate Blogging Corporate blogging is a relatively new idea, and the jury is still out on whether it will succeed.

This controversial marketing tool may be the beginning of a new kind of advertising strategy, or it may fizzle out in a matter of months. Many companies are looking for ways to capitalize on the blogging trend, and many of these corporations have determined that a great way to ride the blogging wave is to keep a blog on their corporate website. These blogs are often created to appeal to the demographic that the company needs to court, and the content may have quite a lot to do with the activities of the corporation, or it may have very little to do with the company itself. Often, a corporate blog will focus on the kinds of content likely to attract the desired surfers, even if that content is not related to the product or service that the company provides. Some bloggers feel that corporate blogging is a kind of validation for the blogging movement, and shows that this exciting new medium has infiltrated the mainstream. Other bloggers consider the kind of viral marketing that corporate blogs practice to be unethical or distasteful. In any case, watching the evolution of corporate blogs and whether they survive and proliferate or fail and disappear promises to provide some interesting insight into today's consumers.

CHAPTER SIX

To Join a Blogging Site or Not to Join

Traffic Sources Getting joins from different sites isn't the best way to draw in guests to visit your blog. This time, we will investigate elective techniques to draw in excellent rush hour gridlock with both free and paid strategies. The principal thing you can do to produce traffic is to reuse all the substance you have composed on your blog. What I truly mean is to transform your blog entries into little "manuals" or articles that assist individuals with taking care of their issues or deal with significant data and submit them to article indexes.

These article catalogs resemble aggregators that gather articles of comparative subjects together in one spot, so they get a great many qualified guests consistently. At the point when you present your articles to these registries, you are presenting your name to the huge number of sets of eyes visiting them for nothing! On most article catalogs, you are likewise allowed to incorporate an "asset box" where you can incorporate your contact subtleties, a straightforward life story, etc. This is the place where you can use the traffic of the said article indexes.

Some great article catalogs to kick you off: www.eZineArticles.com and www.ultimatearticledirectory.comwww.submityourarticle.com One more incredible approach to acquire traffic is to join web discussions that depend on your specialty. To track down these sorts of gatherings, simply go to any web crawler and enter " +forum", without the statements. You would need the most engaged gathering with a generous number of dynamic individuals, and ideally continually clamoring with action. Simply check the dates of the strings posted on the gathering.

At the point when you join dynamic gatherings that emphasize your field of conversation and post extremely helpful and significant posts, your friends will begin seeing you and focusing on what you need to say. In many discussions, you are likewise permitted to attach a connection to your site in the marked line, which is under each post you make on the gatherings. Individuals will snap and visit your blog on the off chance that they discover your posts accommodating and educational. Thusly, your believability is fabricated even before they land on your blog, so traffic from the discussions would be simpler to transform into benefits if your blog is selling your items or suggesting others' as an affiliate since they are as of now persuaded no doubt about it in the field.

The procedure we'll talk about is verbal. Suppose you as of now have an everyday guest count of 100. Imagine a scenario in which you aggregated a little report or gift and posted it on your blog, saying that if a specific guest can allude three of his/her companions to visit your blog the gift will be his/hers for nothing. On the off chance that your little report or gift is sufficiently rewarding, it will create a little buzz among your blog perusers and they will most likely allude to their companions to this blog that they are continuous! You can likewise use the "blog and ping" procedure that everybody's discussing.

Essentially, when you update your blog, you can let blog entries, for example, www.technorati.com know by pinging them. You can ping a ton of entries without a moment's delay by utilizing the free www.pingomatic.com. Other than the procedures depicted here, there are additionally paid techniques like purchasing joins from high-positioning pages or purchasing standard promotion space. A thing to remember when purchasing paid traffic is to consistently gauge your benefits produced from the paid promotions. On the off chance that your benefits do not counterbalance the cost, you will wind up losing cash, so pick shrewdly.

CHAPTER SEVEN

Successful Blog Marketing Tips

So you have a blog and want to market it and make it a successful blog. How do you do this? How do you go about getting your blog out there to be seen and known by others? How do you draw readers and keep them coming back for more? There are many ways to get your blog out there and known by others. This can be known as challenging for some and just quite easy for others. If you have ever had a successful blog before then you know what it takes. You are not going to get anywhere by just setting up a blog and hoping that people will find it and read it. You are not going to gain any links, or a higher search engine ranking by just having a blog. This is all part of blog marketing. Anyone can do it, even you.

Successful blog marketing tip number one. When you first create a blog, of course, it is unheard of. No one knows anything about the blog unless you give them the link and show it to them. However, for a new blog that has never been seen, there are many ways to get it out there and known. You just need to know-how. The first thing that you can do is to allow RSS feeds to be taken from your blog. Allow other websites and blogs to publish your same blog. When you do this, they are giving you a link back to your blog, and also telling their readers all about your blog. You will get more traffic than ever with this tool. RSS feeds are wonderful for promoting and getting your blog out there.

Blog marketing tip number two. Update your blog frequently. We can not put enough emphasis on this trip. If you tell your readers that you are going to update your blog daily, then do it. If you tell them that you will be writing in your blog weekly, don't let them down. Your readers are what makes your blog successful. You may not realize this in the beginning, and you will have few readers in the beginning as well, but you will eventually build a readership base and have people checking out your blog regularly.

Maybe you do not plan on telling your readers how often you will update your blog. That is ok too. However, think about this, if you were reading a blog every week, and you expected to see the blog that you like to read updated at least once a week, you would be very disappointed to find out that it was not. Sure, things happen that might prevent you from updating, and that is expected, and excused, but week after week can hurt you and cause you to lose readers.

Tip number three. While you are working on your readership base and trying to gain readers, you are going to find that commenting on blogs that are relevant to yours will surely help. Find a blog that is on the same topic as yours, or close to it and leave comments. You can also make a trackback with your blog postings to comment on your blog. Doing so will probably more than likely give someone else the urge to track back to your blog. Which will be good for it as well. Commenting on blogs that get many comments will make you be seen by those interested in that market. You will gain traffic and readers that way, and it is easy as well as free.

The fourth blog marketing tip. Learn and apply SEO to your blogs. SEO is search engine optimization. You are going to find that if you want your blog to go anywhere, you need SEO, and you need to know how to use it to the advantage of your blog. Just like a website, a blog will be better off optimized.

9 798886 294514

Printed by Libri Plureos GmbH in Hamburg,
Germany